Truth Deco

How AI Fights Fake News in a Digital Age

Taylor Royce

DEDICATION

To everyone who looks for the truth, dispels false information, and works nonstop to create a world that is more open and knowledgeable. This is a book for the teachers who encourage critical thinking, the technologists who innovate ethically, the legislators who formulate laws with vision, and the people who defend the value of information.

To the innumerable voices heard and unheard that work to guarantee that the truth wins out in this uncertain era. May we keep collaborating to protect the accuracy of information, give one another the skills to separate fact from fiction, and create a future in which knowledge advances society.

Because truth is worth the struggle, this book is for everyone who believes in the power of well-informed decision-making, including doubters, visionaries, dreamers, and doers.

DISCLAIMER

The information contained in this book is meant solely for educational purposes. The author's thoughts, opinions, and insights are their own and may not represent those of any institution, organization, or other entity with whom the author may have affiliations.

Although every attempt has been taken to guarantee the quality and dependability of the material supplied, neither the author nor the publisher expressly nor implicitly offer any guarantees or assurances about the content's completeness, accuracy, or applicability. It is advised that readers independently confirm the material and, where necessary, consult a specialist, particularly when it comes to legal, medical, or technological issues.

The reader bears all liability for the use of any information in this book. Any losses resulting directly or indirectly from the use of this content are not the responsibility of the publisher or the author.

External resources, links, or references to websites

belonging to third parties are not intended to imply support or approval of the information or opinions presented therein.

CONTENTS

Truth Decoded

9

ACKNOWLEDGMENTS

To everyone who helped to create and finish this book, I would like to extend my sincere gratitude. I am lucky to have had the encouragement and support of numerous people along this trip, which has been both gratifying and challenging.

I want to start by expressing my gratitude to my family and friends for their patience and constant support. I sincerely appreciate your love and support, and your confidence in me has been a continual source of inspiration.

To my mentors and coworkers, thank you for your helpful advice, comments, and ideas that have greatly influenced this work. The range and depth of the information provided here have been enhanced by your kind sharing of your knowledge, which I greatly appreciate.

Additionally, I want to thank the numerous scholars, professionals, and institutions whose work has influenced and shaped the concepts in these pages. It is incredibly motivating to see the combined expertise and commitment of the international community to combating the problems of disinformation and developing AI.

Lastly, I want to express my sincere gratitude to my readers. Your interest and participation motivate me to keep researching these important subjects. I believe that the concepts presented in this book will lead to fresh discussions, encourage more research, and support the continuous endeavor to manage and influence the information landscape.

I appreciate everyone's participation in this adventure.

Truth Decoded

CHAPTER 1

COMPREHENDING THE FAKE NEWS SCENARIO

1.1 How Misinformation Develops

False information is not a recent development. Although its impact has undoubtedly been amplified and hastened by the internet, fake news has its origins in human history and is ingrained in our battles for ideology, power, control, and influence. We must comprehend the complex historical background of false news as well as how contemporary technology has altered its effectiveness if we are to fully comprehend the current issue.

Examining the Historical Foundations of Disinformation and Propaganda

Even before the printing press and the internet, there was fake news. In the past, persons in positions of authority have used disinformation as a calculated tactic to sway public opinion, engender fear, control narratives, and defend political choices.

- Prehistoric Societies: Mark Antony was the target of infamous slanderous propaganda in ancient Rome by Octavian (later Augustus Caesar), who portrayed him as a traitor who was influenced by the Egyptian queen Cleopatra. This story was crucial in influencing Roman popular opinion and providing justification for war.

- Disputes over Religion: Both Protestant and Catholic groups disseminated inflammatory pamphlets with inflated or untrue claims in an effort to weaken the opposition during the Protestant Reformation. One of the first scalable false news artifacts were these early printed documents, which were manufactured in large quantities using the Gutenberg press.

- Propaganda during the War: Fake news was methodically established during the world wars in the 20th century. To deceive enemy armies and maintain their own populations in line with national goals, governments employed radio broadcasts, posters, and controlled press sources. For example, exaggerated accounts of enemy atrocities were often published to justify military violence.

These instances highlight an important fact: fake news has always developed in tandem with communication technologies. Its goal of misleading, persuading, and polarizing people doesn't vary, even though its form does.

How Disinformation Strategies Were Changed by Technology

Not only has the shift from print to digital media altered the scope of disinformation, but it has completely transformed it.

- Reach and Speed: What was once a laborious, manual procedure has become an instantaneous worldwide phenomenon thanks to the internet and social media. These days, fake news can reach millions of people in a matter of hours.

- Decentralization and anonymity: In the past,

publication came with more personal responsibility and required access to press facilities. Nowadays, almost anybody can produce and share content anonymously, which makes it easier for false information to proliferate.

- AI Manipulation and Deepfakes: Artificial intelligence-generated articles, deepfake movies, and synthetic audio are some of the new types of fake material that have emerged with the development of AI. In ways that are frequently indistinguishable to the human eye and ear, these technologies blur the boundaries between reality and fiction.

- Algorithmic Amplification: Because social media and search engines are designed to maximize engagement and revenue, they frequently inadvertently give preference to information that is sensational or divisive. Because misinformation is controversial, it naturally flourishes in this ecology.

Even though people have always had the desire to lie, the resources at our disposal today make fake news more harmful and challenging to stop than in the past.

1.2 The Fake News Anatomy

Examining the construction of fake news is essential to comprehending what makes it credible. Fake news is rarely just lies; it's a well-planned concoction of emotional appeals, partial facts, and persuasive strategies that take advantage of human nature and structural flaws in the way information is disseminated.

Features, Organizations, and Trends of False Content

Although these characteristics can be minor and easy to miss, fake news frequently has unique characteristics that set it apart from authentic journalism.

- Triggers for emotions: They are characterized by emotionally charged language, sensational headlines, and claims that make people angry. These automatically captivate the reader, increasing the likelihood that they will spread the information without question.

- Targeting for Confirmation Bias: A target audience's preexisting opinions are frequently supported by fake news. As a result, readers feel validated and are more inclined to share the content, creating a reinforcing loop.

- Visual Misdirection: Using Photoshopped photos, deceptive graphs, or fake video clips gives the message more legitimacy while concealing its dishonesty.

- Pseudo-sources and False Attribution: In order to look authentic, a lot of fake news articles use fictitious experts, unreliable "inside sources," or imitate the design of reliable news sites.

- The binary framing method Fake news frequently simplifies complex topics into binary terms, erasing complexity and fostering divisiveness.

These frameworks are intentionally designed to be believable and contagious.

Differentiating Between False, False, and Malinformation

Differentiating between related but different types of deceptive content is crucial:

- Misinformation: Inaccurate or misleading information disseminated without malicious intent. Example: Thinking it's true, a friend spreads a misleading health suggestion.

- Disinformation: Willfully inaccurate information disseminated with the intention of misleading or controlling. For instance, political smear campaigns or propaganda supported by the state.

- Malinformation: Technically accurate information that is misused, frequently without context, or with the intent to cause harm. Example: Discrediting people by leaking confidential emails or papers.

The reaction plan is informed by these distinctions, which

makes them significant. Not all misleading content is intentionally produced, and knowing intent makes countermeasures more accurate.

1.3 The Effects of Fake News on Society

Fake news is a disruptive force that has serious repercussions for democracy, social trust, public safety, and economic stability. It is not a benign byproduct of the digital age.

Cultural, Political, and Economic Repercussions

- Erosion of Democratic Institutions: The public's capacity to make educated decisions is weakened by fake news. As seen in several democratic countries throughout the past ten years, election-related misinformation can affect voter turnout, legitimacy perceptions, and even spark unrest.

- Polarization and Social Fragmentation: People may enter echo chambers where they only ingest information that confirms their prejudices as a result of false narratives. This exacerbates social divisions and increases animosity between groups.

- Public Health Risks: False information regarding vaccinations, therapies, and the characteristics of the virus itself could have fatal consequences during the COVID-19 pandemic. Misinformation caused people to be reluctant to get vaccines, turn to risky home cures, and oppose public health initiatives.

- Economic Sabotage: Financial markets may be impacted by false information. Stock market swings and investor fear have been brought on by false claims regarding businesses, mergers, or national policy.

- Cultural Manipulation: Hate crimes, xenophobia, and strained diplomatic ties have all been caused by false narratives that attack nations, faiths, or ethnic groups.

Real-World Damage Case Studies

- Pizzagate (2016): A man used a rifle to enter a pizzeria in Washington, D.C., after a conspiracy theory erroneously claimed that Democratic leaders and a child-trafficking network were connected to the establishment. Although there were no casualties, the incident demonstrated how misinformation spread online may incite violence in the real world.

- Lynchings by WhatsApp Mobs in India, 2017–2018: WhatsApp was used to send viral bogus messages regarding kidnappers of children, which resulted in multiple mob violent incidents and multiple fatalities. The platform's decentralized structure made containment challenging, even in the face of repeated official warnings.

- Stock Market Hoaxes: A bogus report that United Airlines was going bankrupt went viral online in 2008, sending the company's stock plunging sharply before trading was stopped.

Fake news has the power to harm, deceive, and even kill

people, as these incidents illustrate.

1.4 The Rapid Spread of False Information

We can improve our defenses by comprehending the mechanisms behind the spread of bogus news. Strong digital systems and ingrained psychological habits are the main causes of the speed and extent of the transmission of false information.

Psychological Drivers and Cognitive Biases

- Confirmation Bias: Regardless of the truthfulness of information, people are more likely to believe and spread it if it supports their preconceived notions.

- Availability Heuristic: Information that is highly visible or easily remembered is frequently taken for granted. Regular exposure to a lie makes it seem more true; this phenomenon is called "illusory truth."

- Social Proof: People are more likely to believe and

spread content if others in their network are doing so.

- Fear and Outrage: Information that makes people feel scared, angry, or shocked spreads more quickly. These feelings are strong inducers of action, including clicking "share."

- Cognitive Ease: Even if a message is untrue, it is more likely to be believed if it is clear and easy to understand than if it is complex.

The Function of Algorithmic Amplification and Social Media

- Algorithms Based on Engagement: Content that receives likes, comments, and shares is given priority on social media sites like Facebook, YouTube, and X (previously Twitter). Because fake news is designed to evoke strong emotions, it frequently performs better than actual news in these criteria.

- Virality Loops: Digital platforms are designed to spread quickly. In only a few minutes, a single post can generate thousands of shares, disseminating false information at a speed that human fact-checkers cannot match.

- Filter Bubbles: Algorithms create secluded environments where users only see narratives that reinforce one another by tailoring content feeds based on historical behavior. This seclusion restricts access to correcting information and feeds polarization.

- Incentives for Monetization: Fake news websites frequently use advertisements and rely on traffic to generate income. This generates a financial incentive to aggressively manufacture and disseminate misleading content.

The proliferation of fake news is not solely due to people's ignorance, but also to the way that digital environments and psychological traits are designed to support it.

It takes a sophisticated understanding of historical context, psychological weaknesses, and technology enablers to comprehend false news, which goes beyond just spotting lies. The foundation for examining the fake news situation from several angles, its development, composition, effects, and dissemination has been established by this chapter. Understanding the battlefield is half the battle in the pursuit of truth

CHAPTER 2

CONVENTIONAL METHODS FOR IDENTIFYING FALSE NEWS

Identifying and preventing false news has become essential to preserving democracy, public discourse, and social trust as the digital information landscape continues to expand in scope and complexity. The foundation for how we recognize and react to misinformation and disinformation was established by conventional techniques prior to the development of advanced machine learning algorithms and artificial intelligence. Although these fundamental methods are based on reason and good intentions, they also have drawbacks that need to be recognized and interpreted in their proper context.

The effectiveness, drawbacks, and historical development of the traditional methods used to identify fake news are examined in this chapter.

2.1 Manual Techniques for Verifying Facts

The function of independent fact-checkers and journalists

Truth-seeking was the purview of journalists, editors, and investigative researchers long before "fake news" spread like wildfire online. In order to ensure accurate reporting, human specialists manually fact-check claims by comparing them to reliable sources, confirming facts against records, and examining context.

Companies like:

- PolitiFact
- Snopes
- FactCheck.org
- The International Fact-Checking Network (IFCN) of the Poynter Institute

...have been leading the way in formalized fact-checking. Usually, their procedure entails:

- Finding a claim that has drawn interest or attention from the general public.
- Confirming the claim's context and place of origin.
- Examining the assertion in light of reliable sources (such as government publications and peer-reviewed journals).
- Depending on the organization, publishing a thorough investigation with a conclusion that ranges from "true" to "false" or even "pants on fire."

Advantages

- Credibility and Trust: These techniques are highly authoritative and frequently seen as trustworthy by the general public.
- Contextual Nuance: Human fact-checkers are able to take historical, political, and cultural context into account, something that algorithms frequently overlook.
- Accountability: The public and media are held more accountable due to the transparency of their procedures.

Restrictions

- Labor-Intensive: Manual fact-checking requires a lot of time and resources.
- Reactive, Not Proactive: A claim may have already gained widespread attention by the time it is validated.
- Bias Perception: Even neutral organizations can be accused of bias, especially in highly polarized environments.
- Scalability Issues: It is unrealistic to fact-check everything due to the vast volume of daily output.

The incapacity of manual fact-checking to keep up with real-time misinformation poses a significant difficulty in the digital age, despite the fact that it is important, particularly for politically sensitive or high-impact information.

2.2 Heuristic and Rule-Based Models

Preliminary Computational Detection Attempts

As internet content became more prevalent, researchers and developers started creating rule-based systems to automatically identify false information. These systems categorize data using pre-established heuristics or logical rules. For instance:

- News stories with sensationalist language or no citations may be reported. Content from known dubious websites may be automatically labeled or deprioritized. As warning signs for possible lies, linguistic cues like exaggeration, excessive punctuation (!!!), or emotionally charged words are employed.

Typical characteristics of rule-based detection include:

- Keyword matching (e.g., "miracle cure," "hoax").
- Scores for readability Non-journalistic purposes may be indicated by extremely low or high scores.
- Source credibility lists (known domains' white or blacklists).
- Articles that lack substance and have clickbait headlines are considered to have a poor content

structure.

Restrictions in Multilingual and Dynamic Environments

Despite being novel at the time, rule-based and heuristic models are ineffective in complex, contemporary situations for a number of reasons.

- Rigidity: These systems are difficult to adjust. The rules are easy for fake news producers to pick up and adapt to.
- Lack of Contextual Understanding: Because algorithms take sarcasm or irony literally, they may identify it as fake news.
- Multilingual Difficulties: Heuristics frequently depend on verbal cues that are difficult to communicate between languages.
- False Positives/Negatives: Oversimplified models may miss subtle misinformation or incorrectly label honest stuff.

Notwithstanding these limitations, rule-based systems

played a crucial role in demonstrating the feasibility of automated detection, paving the way for more flexible solutions.

2.3 Methods Based on Crowdsourcing

Using Human Networks for Information Verification

Crowd-sourced techniques depend on big populations of internet users to evaluate and identify potentially misleading content. Community feedback has been used by websites such as Wikipedia, Reddit, and even Facebook (to a certain extent) to edit or validate content.

Important instances:

- Wikipedia's editorial model: Thousands of users keep an eye on edits in real time, swiftly removing inaccurate material as they are discovered.
- Facebook's previous third-party verification program: Content was reported by community members and forwarded to fact-checkers.
- Subreddit guidelines for Reddit moderation:

Community moderators frequently enforce honesty and quality standards.

The advantages of crowdsourcing

- Large user bases can jointly monitor enormous volumes of content thanks to Scalability: Diverse viewpoints and cultural interpretations can be contributed by individuals with varying backgrounds.
- Speed: Institutional fact-checkers may not react as quickly as certain communities.

Difficulties and Restrictions

- Reliability Issues: The quality of the crowd determines the accuracy of the truth gathered from it. Falsehoods can be reinforced by echo chambers.
- Biases and Manipulation: Coordinated attempts (bribery, vote manipulation) can skew perceptions of reality.
- Sustainability Concerns: Long-term efficacy may be weakened by user exhaustion, burnout, or a lack of

incentives.

- Moderation Gaps: Some platforms lack the strong infrastructure for moderation necessary to manage complex content.

Crowd-sourcing can improve community involvement and alertness, but it is susceptible to manipulation and lacks the accuracy required for sensitive or important information screening.

2.4 Issues with Conventional Approaches

Despite their unique advantages, conventional methods of identifying false news have several basic issues that have reduced their effectiveness in the fast-paced, information-rich digital world of today.

Speed and Scalability Limitations

- Volume Overload: Every day, millions of postings, videos, and articles are produced. It is not feasible for manual and rule-based systems to stay up.
- Latency: Content may have been viewed or shared

thousands, if not millions, of times before it is confirmed or refuted.

- Human Resource Limitations: Given the global reach of false information, even the biggest fact-checking groups have a small workforce and few resources.

Adapting to changing narratives can be challenging.

- Quick Changes in False Narratives: Adaptive propaganda, repackaged hoaxes, and conspiracy theories appear more often than static detection rules.
- Linguistic and Cultural Diversity: Cultural sensitivity and linguistic processing are both necessary for effective false news detection. In multilingual settings, traditional approaches frequently fall short.
- Visual Misinformation: A large portion of today's misinformation is disseminated through edited photos or movies, which are inaccessible through conventional text-based techniques.
- Decentralization of Content Creation: It is getting

harder to pinpoint the original sources of false information as independent influencers and user-generated content platforms proliferate.

The following are additional constraints:

- Ethical and Legal Difficulties: Platforms may be reluctant to vigorously filter content out of concern that it would violate free speech.
- Platform Limitations: The ability and willingness of various platforms to put in place stringent fake news detection systems varies.
- Trust Erosion: Persistent accusations of bias or agenda-driven fact-checking can erode public confidence, making these initiatives less successful.

The way society recognizes and reacts to misleading information has been largely defined by traditional methods of detecting fake news. These approaches, which range from the painstaking labor of human fact-checkers to the earliest computational tools and crowd-driven models, have all produced insightful frameworks. Nevertheless, these traditional systems have increasing constraints in terms of scale, adaptability, and credibility as disinformation strategies get more complex and rapid.

These legacy systems' shortcomings do not diminish their worth; rather, they emphasize the need for more creative, flexible, and cooperative methods in the continuous search for the truth. By being aware of the shortcomings of previous approaches, we can better plan and support future solutions that can handle the complexity and scope of the current digital information environment.

CHAPTER 3

Artificial Intelligence Foundations in Fake News Detection

Media verification is only one of the many businesses that have undergone radical change with the introduction of artificial intelligence (AI). Traditional detection methods have proven inadequate to handle the scope and complexity of the problem as false news and misinformation have continued to grow. AI provides a flexible and scalable system that can process enormous volumes of data in real-time, spot trends, and forecast false information with an efficiency that manual approaches cannot match. This chapter explores in detail the fundamentals of artificial intelligence (AI) technologies, particularly machine learning (ML) and natural language processing (NLP), as they apply to the identification of false news.

3.1 Overview of Natural Language Processing, AI, and Machine Learning

Understanding the fundamental ideas underlying AI technology is essential to appreciating their role in the fight against fake news.

Fundamental Ideas and Words

- Artificial Intelligence (AI): A vast area of computer science concerned with developing machines that can carry out operations that normally call for human intelligence. Reasoning, learning, decision-making, perception, and language comprehension are some of these tasks.

- Machine Learning (ML: A branch of artificial intelligence in which algorithms are not explicitly designed but instead learn from data to produce predictions or judgments. As more data becomes accessible, machine learning (ML) adjusts and gets better, which is very helpful in the constantly shifting false news landscape.

- Deep Learning (DL): An additional subset of machine learning that uses multi-layered neural networks—thus the term "deep"—to represent intricate correlations in data. When it comes to tasks like picture identification and complex language modeling, DL excels.

- Natural Language Processing (NLP: An area of artificial intelligence that focuses on how computers and human language interact. Machines can read, comprehend, interpret, and produce human language thanks to natural language processing (NLP). Analyzing news stories, tweets, blog entries, and other text-based content starts with this.

Distinctions Among ML, DL, and NLP in the Context of Fake News

When it comes to spotting fake news, each of these domains offers special skills:

- The framework for identifying patterns in both

labeled and unlabeled data is provided by ML. For example, ML algorithms are trained to categorize future news items by feeding in thousands of articles that have been classified as "real" or "fake."

- DL provides more depth by identifying high-level characteristics in intricate datasets. For instance, deep learning models such as transformers (e.g., BERT, GPT) are able to comprehend language's semantic context and subtleties that more straightforward machine learning models might overlook.

- NLP is essential for tokenizing, parsing, sentiment analysis, and meaning extraction from text. NLP algorithms are able to recognize emotionally charged or manipulative language in articles as possible warning signs for false content.

These technologies frequently cooperate. A machine learning model may be used to classify the data once features are extracted and preprocessed by an NLP module. They work together to create a pipeline that can detect bogus news with confidence.

3.2 Data: AI Models' Fuel

Without data, no AI system can function effectively. The type, quality, and labeling of data are critical factors that impact any AI model's performance when it comes to detecting fake news.

Data Types Employed

1. Text Information:

- Headlines, blog posts, tweets, articles, and captions The majority of fake news datasets are composed of text data, which necessitates a great deal of preprocessing and analysis.

2. Image Information:

- Visual elements like images, graphs, and memes that are affixed to news stories Artificial intelligence (AI) algorithms are able to identify discrepancies, photoshopped photographs, or deceptive imagery linked to fraudulent information.

3. Metadata:

• Details regarding the author, URL, publishing date, and source. Particularly in articles produced by bots, metadata is essential for identifying trends in information distribution and tracking its source.

Issues with Data Quality, Annotation, and Bias

Quality of Data:
Effective models require data that is balanced, clean, and well-structured. Model accuracy can be weakened by noise, irregularities, and unbalanced datasets.

Difficulties with Annotation:
Data about bogus news is difficult to categorize. Expert judgment, contextual knowledge, and temporal awareness are frequently needed to determine ground truth. Annotators need to distinguish between purposeful disinformation, opinion, parody, and satire.

Bias Concerns:

Biases in the data are inherited by AI models. For instance, the model can unjustly learn to link particular political organizations' ideology with false information if the training data contains more fake news from those groups, producing biased results. Ensuring representative and diverse datasets is crucial.

To create reliable AI systems for detecting fake news, proper data governance curation, documentation, validation, and ethical oversight is essential.

3.3 Methods of Training and Validation

Teaching an AI model to recognize patterns in past data and extrapolate those patterns to new examples is known as training. The training approach has an effect on the model's dependability and functionality in practical situations.

Learning Under and Under Supervision

Learning Under Supervision:

- Depends on labeled datasets, in which a predicted outcome (such as "fake" or "real") is associated with each instance of input data.

- Typical algorithms include Random Forest, Support Vector Machines (SVM), Neural Networks, and Logistic Regression.

- Benefit: Excellent accuracy when labeled data is abundant and trustworthy.

- Drawback: Needs a lot of hand labeling, which is subjective and resource-intensive.

Learning Without Supervision:

- Utilizes unlabeled data. Without using pre-established categories, the program looks for trends, clusters, or anomalies. Helpful in identifying fresh false material, classifying related articles, or identifying emerging fake news patterns.

- K-means clustering, DBSCAN, and autoencoders are examples of common algorithms.

- Limitation: Less accurate for classification tasks; frequently used in conjunction with supervised techniques.

Reinforcement learning and semi-supervised learning:

A big volume of unlabeled data can be used in conjunction with a modest amount of labeled data using hybrid techniques. Reinforcement learning, however less popular in this sector, may be used to constantly update models based on feedback.

Model tuning, cross-validation, and overfitting

Cross-Checking:

A method for training and testing the model across different combinations that involves dividing the data into multiple subsets. This guarantees that no single train-test split will affect the model's performance. Stratified sampling and k-fold validation are common techniques.

Overfitting:

- A situation in which the model performs poorly

when generalizing to new data because it learns the training data—including its noise and quirks—too well. Low accuracy on test data and high accuracy on training data are symptoms.

- Regularization, dropout (in neural networks), decision tree pruning, and model simplification are among solutions.

Model Adjustment:

- Entails modifying hyperparameters (such as regularization coefficients, learning rate, and number of layers) to maximize model performance.
- Methods: Bayesian optimization, random search, and grid search.

Achieving effective training requires striking a careful balance between avoiding overfitting and discovering significant patterns. To assess success, precise measurements are also necessary.

3.4 Assessing Model Effectiveness

A model must undergo a thorough evaluation after training in order to ascertain its practicality. A number of performance metrics and diagnostic tools are essential to this assessment.

Confusion Matrices, F1-Score, Accuracy, Precision, and Recall

Every metric offers a unique perspective on the model's performance.

- Accuracy: The proportion of instances that were accurately predicted to all instances. Although intuitive, accuracy by itself might be deceptive in datasets that are unbalanced (e.g., when fake news is infrequent).

- Precision: Calculates the percentage of actual positive results among all anticipated positive results. In order to avoid misleading allegations of misinformation, high precision means fewer false positives.

- Remember (Sensitivity): Calculates the percentage of real positives that are true positives. Although the model may occasionally misclassify actual content, high recall indicates that it detects more bogus news.

- F1-Score: the precision and recall harmonic mean. offers a fair metric in situations when detecting more false information and preserving accuracy must be traded off.

- Confusion Matrix: True positives, false positives, true negatives, and false negatives are displayed in a tabular representation of actual versus projected classifications. It is crucial for identifying the model's shortcomings and directing enhancements.

Benchmarking Model Difficulties

Fake news's dynamic nature:
Every day, new strategies, subjects, and language idioms appear. It's possible that models trained on historical data won't function effectively on new material.

Domain Shift:

When used to health-related fake news, a model trained on political misinformation may not perform well, and vice versa.

No standardized datasets are available:

Fair model comparison is challenging due to the lack of widely recognized benchmarks. Results are skewed by differences in task definitions, labeling techniques, and data sources.

Assessment in Real-Time Environments:

Real-world usability may not be reflected in laboratory measures. Operational limitations, user feedback loops, and delay are introduced when models are deployed in newsrooms, platforms, or browsers.

Maintaining model relevance and efficacy frequently requires ongoing observation, retraining, and human-in-the-loop validation.

Modern fake news detection systems are built on artificial intelligence, which is fueled by reliable data and sophisticated algorithms. Stakeholders may make well-informed decisions on the design, implementation, and management of these systems by having a thorough awareness of the technical landscape, which includes machine learning principles, natural language processing capabilities, data dynamics, and performance evaluation. But as time goes on, it becomes more and more obvious that AI is not a panacea. It is an effective but flawed technology that needs to be used carefully, in conjunction with human judgment, and continuously improved to suit the changing demands of digital disinformation

CHAPTER 4

TEXT-BASED DETECTION METHODS

The fight against fake news has shifted more and more into the field of text-based identification as the digital world takes over as the main channel for information distribution. This chapter explores in detail the methods, resources, and knowledge that underpin contemporary fake news detection systems. Building strong protections against disinformation requires an understanding of how machines learn to categorize, evaluate, and analyze language, which frequently forms the first layer of a dishonest article or post.

4.1 Machine Learning-Based Text Classification

The majority of false news detection techniques are based on text categorization. Systems can be trained to distinguish between factual and misleading content with greater accuracy by transforming text into structured data and using machine learning methods. Here, we examine the most popular models and their applications.

Fundamental Text Classification Algorithms

1. The classifier known as Naïve Bayes

This approach, which is well-known for its effectiveness with text data, is based on Bayes' Theorem and presupposes feature independence.

- Benefits: Uses tiny datasets well and is quick to train and forecast.
- Applicable to Fake News: Despite its simplicity, it captures probabilistic correlations in word distributions between fake and authentic news, making it a popular baseline.

2. SVMs (Support Vector Machines)

SVMs seek to identify the best hyperplane dividing classes and are efficient in high-dimensional spaces.

- Advantages: Effective with sparse text features, such as TF-IDF vectors.

- Use in false News: Because of its resilience with text features, it is frequently employed in early stages of false news research.

3. The use of logistic regression

A statistical model that forecasts class membership probabilities.

- Advantages: Computationally efficient and easy to understand.
- Use in Fake News: Perfect for binary classification (actual vs. fake), particularly when features are well-designed.

Classification through Feature Engineering

Raw text needs to be formatted meaningfully in order to be fed into these algorithms efficiently:

- Term Frequency-Inverse Document Frequency, or TF-IDF,
- reduces the weight of frequently used but uninformative terms by allocating weight to words

based on their value across documents.

Sequences of n words or characters are known as N-grams; these enable models to capture context in addition to individual words.

- Bigrams/Trigrams: Word pairs or triplets that capture brief phrases or collocations
- Unigrams: Single words

Cease Lemmatization & Word Removal

For consistency, words are reduced to their most basic forms and common but uninformative terms (such as "the," "is," etc.) are eliminated.

When carefully retrieved and constructed, these features serve as the foundation for machine learning models.

4.2 Text Detection Using Deep Learning Models

Deep learning has allowed systems to learn directly from raw or semi-processed text, capturing semantics and context at a far deeper level than classical machine learning, which excels on structured representations.

GRU and LSTM Recurrent Neural Networks (RNNs)

1. Long Short-Term Memory Networks, or LSTMs

Long-term dependencies in text can be remembered using LSTMs, which were created to solve the vanishing gradient issue in conventional RNNs.

- Application: Determining whether a narrative is consistent or not, as this may indicate that the content is fake.

2. Gated Recurrent Units (GRU)

GRUs, a condensed form of LSTM, retain performance in a variety of applications while being computationally more efficient.

- Application: Because it requires fewer resources, it works well in real-time fake news detection systems.

Text-Based Convolutional Neural Networks (CNNs)

Despite being widely used in image processing, CNNs have shown surprising efficacy in text classification:

- Application: Identifying regional patterns, such as particular words or language clues that point to dishonesty.

Word Inclusions

Deep learning makes use of embeddings that capture semantic meaning, whereas traditional models consider words as discrete tokens.

Based on how words are used in context, Word2Vec transforms them into continuous vectors. A pair of architectures

- Skip-gram: Given a target word, it predicts neighboring words. CBOW: Forecasts a target word based on contextual information.

- Global Vectors for Word Representation, or GloVe captures syntactic and semantic links by using word co-occurrence data throughout the corpus.

Bidirectional Encoder Representations from Transformers, or BERT, is a potent language model with bidirectional text reading and more sophisticated context understanding.

- Application: Because BERT can understand context, sarcasm, and implicit meanings, it is state-of-the-art in many fake news detection tasks.

When attempting to discern between authentic and fake tales, these models allow for a more human-like comprehension of language.

4.3 Stylistic and Linguistic Indications

Subtle cues in human language convey authenticity, tone, and intent. Both linguistic specialists and machine learning systems can identify and analyze the telltale style indicators found in deceptive literature.

Emotional Tone and Sentiment

Emotional Evaluation

Exaggerated feelings, whether good or negative, can be used by fake news to elicit responses.

- For instance, alarmist terms like "unbelievable," "devastating," or "terrifying" may be used in fake news.

Detection of Emotions

Emotions that are frequently used in false material to increase its virality, such fear, rage, or joy, can be detected by tools.

Analysis of Writing Style

- Lexical Richness: The vocabulary used in real news is typically more varied. Fake news may use bad grammar or repeat emotionally charged phrases.

- Passive Voice: Passive constructions are frequently used in fake news to evade accountability ("It is believed that..." rather than "Experts believe...").

- Clickbait and Hyperbole: Phraseological devices that encourage interest or exaggerate ("You won't believe what happened...").

Linguistic Deceptive Patterns

High Subjectivity
Opinions that are presented as facts are frequently a major component of fake articles.

Factual Anchoring Limited
Articles may rely on anecdotal evidence or anonymous statements in place of credible sources or data points.

Excessive use of punctuation and capitalization
A lack of professionalism and an effort to attract attention might be shown by the overuse of ALL CAPS or several exclamation points.

Detection systems can more accurately determine if an article's goal is to enlighten or to deceive by measuring certain stylistic characteristics.

4.4 Text-Based Detection Case Studies

Applications in the real world offer priceless insights into the practical workings of text-based detection techniques as well as the ongoing difficulties they encounter.

1. The FNC-1 Fake News Challenge

- Goal: Indicate whether the body of a news piece agrees, disagrees, discusses, or is unrelated to a particular headline.
- Method: used a combination of gradient boosting, TF-IDF, and SVM models.
- Result: Showed how crucial stance detection is for spotting subtle disinformation.

2. Identification of COVID-19 Misinformation

A spike in false information about health during the pandemic led to the quick development of detection systems:

- BERT-based classifiers trained on health news

datasets are the models. The challenges are as follows:

- Ambiguity brought on by changing scientific knowledge; Requirement for real-time, multilingual classification.

3. Use of LIAR Datasets

- Description: Contains brief political statements that have been characterized as false, barely truthful, pants-on-fire, etc.
- Importance: gives models a detailed classification system to work with.

Notes:

A balanced class distribution improves the performance of models trained on this dataset. When data is scarce, linguistic features alone can occasionally perform better than neural models.

Present Restrictions and Research Deficits

Despite progress, there are still significant obstacles to

overcome:

- Domain Transferability: A model that has been trained on one kind of content (political news, for example) might not do well on another (health disinformation, for example).

- Bias in Training Data: The biases of platforms or fact-checkers are frequently reflected in the data, which may affect the fairness of the model.

- Explainability: Although BERT and other deep models are strong, they frequently function as "black boxes," making it challenging to defend choices.

To fill in these gaps:

Researchers are investigating technologies that are explainable AI (XAI). Multilingual, more extensive datasets are being created. Newsroom settings are testing hybrid systems that mix human monitoring and machine learning.

At the nexus of language, psychology, and computer intelligence is text-based fake news identification. In order to create systems that can extract meaning, intent, and dishonesty from digital text, researchers and developers continue to use a variety of methods, ranging from conventional classifiers to state-of-the-art neural networks. Even while no system is perfect, the increasing complexity of these methods gives promise in the battle against the flood of false information that defines the digital age. With the smart use of text analytics and artificial intelligence, the difficult path from unprocessed words to actionable truth is becoming easier to traverse

CHAPTER 5

MULTIMODAL DETECTION STRATEGIES

Traditional text-based detection methods are no longer adequate to combat the increasing complexity of digital deception as the dissemination of false information keeps changing. Misinformation is frequently disseminated in multimedia formats, which contain not just text but also pictures, videos, and metadata, in today's media environment. This chapter examines the effectiveness of multimodal detection techniques, which combine several data sources, in thwarting coordinated inauthentic behavior, deepfakes, fake news, and manipulated media. We can create more comprehensive and reliable detection algorithms that surpass the drawbacks of single-mode detection methods by utilizing the interactions between text, photos, videos, and metadata.

5.1 Going Past Text: Identifying False Pictures and Videos

Although text-based strategies have become more popular in the battle against false information, visual materials like pictures and videos frequently have greater persuasive power. The proliferation of deepfakes, manipulated photos, and videos have increased the demand for sophisticated methods that can identify visual disinformation.

Visual Misinformation, Manipulated Media, and Deepfakes

Deepfakes are artificial intelligence (AI)-generated or modified material (pictures or videos) intended to deceive viewers by putting a person's voice or likeness in an inappropriate setting. Convincing fake media is now easier than ever thanks to AI-driven technologies that employ strategies like generative adversarial networks (GANs).

Deepfakes Types:

- The most popular type of deepfake is called a

"face-swapping deepfake," in which the visage of one person is superimposed on that of another.

- Audio deepfakes: voices produced by AI that imitate people or prominent figures.
- Full-body deepfakes: These are more complex deepfakes that use whole bodies rather than simply faces.

From basic edits like cropping and color adjustments to more intricate changes like digitally inserted objects or entire scenes, manipulated photos and videos can include a variety of changes. Because these modifications might be subtle, it can be challenging to detect them.

- Impact of Visual Misinformation: In times of crisis, social unrest, or political manipulation, fake photos and videos are frequently utilized. Visuals are especially good in rapidly disseminating false information because they often have an instantaneous effect.

AI-Powered Multimedia Analysis Tools

An increasing number of AI-driven technologies are being created to counter the proliferation of visual misrepresentation, including deepfakes. These technologies examine multimedia content using a range of methods to spot minute differences that point to tampering.

Technologies for Deepfake Detection:

- Convolutional Neural Networks (CNNs): These networks are very good at spotting anomalies in image and video data at the pixel level. CNNs are used to identify irregular facial expressions, uneven illumination, and misaligned lip motions in recordings.
- Audio-visual cross-checking: AI may check for synchronization issues or incompatibilities in deepfake videos by comparing the audio and visual components.
- Facial Recognition Algorithms: These technologies cross-reference people's faces with databases to identify faces that are edited or mismatched in order to confirm the identities of people in films.
- Image Manipulation Detection: AI models that have

been trained on enormous datasets of both actual and modified images can assist in spotting irregularities like strange noise, odd pixels, or uneven compression artifacts. Images that have been manipulated can be identified with the use of tools such as Photoshop forensic analysis and image splicing detection.

5.2 Integrating Metadata, Image, and Text

While separate techniques for text, image, and video detection are important, combining these modalities to create a more complete and precise detection system is where the true strength lies. Multimodal fusion models can identify small connections and discrepancies that might be missed when examining a single data source separately by utilizing the synergy of text, visual content, and metadata.

Fusion Models and How Well They Work

- Fusion models integrate text, image, and video aspects into a single system, enabling a more thorough comprehension of the validity of the content. The idea behind these models is that several kinds of data might provide complementing insights regarding the content's nature.

- Neural Networks with Multiple Modes: These sophisticated networks simultaneously learn from a variety of input kinds. A system might, for example, examine an article's text, the metadata related to the content, and the visual signals in any accompanying photos or videos. Fusion models can increase the overall detection accuracy and cross-verify content across several modalities by merging these features.

- Text and Visual Alignment: For instance, if an article talks about a political event, the pictures that go with it should match the article's tone and subject matter. Misinformation may be indicated by text and visual discrepancies (for example, a story describing a calm protest with pictures of violent altercations).

- Multimodal Transformers: These deep learning topologies allow text, image, and video processing to be done in a single framework. For example, CLIP

(Contrastive Language-Image Pretraining) use joint embeddings to comprehend both images and text, allowing one to determine whether the image confirms or refutes the text.

Cross-Modal Relationships and Temporal Patterns

The term "temporal patterns" describes how some information changes throughout time. Misinformation and fake news frequently follow certain patterns, such planned social media posting or quick viral propagation. Systems can identify unusual patterns linked to inauthentic conduct by examining the time and order of content posts.

- The inconsistencies between the text and multimedia information can be identified by examining their relationship, for example, if a phony news story is accompanied by an edited image or a deceptive video. This calls for complex models that can comprehend the interactions between many modalities (text, image, and video) inside a single story or event.

- Behavioral Analysis: By comparing the creation and publication dates of an image or video with the textual content, it is possible to identify efforts at real-time information manipulation. Coordinated disinformation campaigns may be indicated, for instance, by abrupt changes in social media activity or a surge in viral material surrounding a certain post.

5.3 Network Analysis and Social Context

The study of social networks he venues where false information is disseminated is one of the best methods for identifying and evaluating fake news. Finding out how false information spreads and whether attempts are being made to control or coordinate information flows can be accomplished by examining the social context and network patterns.

Researching the Spread of False Information on Social Networks

- Social Network Dynamics: False information

frequently spreads more quickly and extensively than accurate information, particularly when it is sensational or emotionally charged. Understanding how false information spreads from a small number of users to a much broader audience can be aided by social network research. Researchers can determine the sources of erroneous information and pinpoint the influential nodes (people) disseminating it by looking at how information moves via social networks like Facebook, Twitter, and Reddit.

- Virality and Emotional Content: Studies have indicated that content with strong emotional appeal has a higher chance of becoming viral. Strong emotional reactions like hatred, fear, or indignation are frequently triggered by fake news, especially misinformation. Detection algorithms can identify questionable trends that might point to the existence of fake news by examining social media reactions (likes, shares, and comments).

Recognizing Coordinated False Conduct

- Coordinated Campaigns: Coordinated inauthentic behavior (CIB) is frequently the cause of fake news, which doesn't necessarily spread naturally. This entails a number of actors collaborating to spread a misleading story. By examining the behavior of several accounts that share identical content or exhibit comparable patterns of activity (e.g., coordinated posting at specified times), AI technologies can identify CIB.

- Bot Detection: Bots, automated accounts that disseminate content at scale, frequently exploit social networks. Artificial intelligence (AI) systems can detect and flag questionable accounts as possible bots by examining user behavior patterns (such as post frequency, account creation time, and absence of human contact).

- Fake Accounts and Trolls: Like bots, trolls are people or organizations that purposefully disseminate false information in an effort to influence politics or society. AI is able to detect odd behavior, such as accounts that aggressively manipulate content or submit misleading content on a regular basis.

5.4 Using Multimodal AI in Real-World Applications

The foundation of many contemporary false news detection systems is the mixing of many data kinds, including text, photos, videos, and metadata. These technologies offer scalable, real-time solutions for detecting fraudulent content in a range of media by utilizing multimodal AI.

Complete Detection Systems

The goal of end-to-end detection platforms is to provide a complete solution for spotting false information in text, photos, and videos. These platforms combine a number of AI models into a single pipeline that can process various content kinds and cross-check them with data from various sources.

Platform Examples:

- Deepware Scanner: A program that analyzes audio

and visual data to find deepfakes.

- TruePic: A platform that instantly confirms the legitimacy of images and movies using blockchain technology and artificial intelligence.

Real-Time Detection: Thanks to developments in artificial intelligence, false information may now be identified and flagged as it circulates across platforms. Governments, social media companies, and news organizations utilize these systems to keep an eye on the information flow and respond when needed.

Illustrations from Industry and Research

- Research: To increase detection accuracy and scalability, multimodal detection systems are continuously improved in academic contexts. Studies have indicated that when text and visual data are combined, fake news detection algorithms perform better overall than when text is used alone.

Applications in Industry:

- Social Media: To identify and stop the spread of false information, businesses such as Facebook and Twitter are creating multimodal detection systems that look at postings and multimedia content.

- News Media: To stop the spread of false information in breaking stories, news outlets are employing AI-based technologies to swiftly validate photos and videos.

Multimodal detection techniques are a potent way to combat the constantly changing misinformation situation. AI systems are able to identify minor differences that would otherwise go undetected by merging various data sources, such as text, photos, videos, and metadata. More precise, effective, and scalable ways to counteract fake news are made possible by the integration of these various information sources. The capacity to counteract textual and visual disinformation in real-time will grow as we continue to create increasingly complex multimodal models, offering a potent weapon in the battle against the ubiquitous menace of bogus material

CHAPTER 6

SYSTEMS AND APPLICATIONS IN THE REAL WORLD

The spread of false information in this era of information overload has made creative remedies imperative. In the fight against the dissemination of misleading information, artificial intelligence (AI) has become a potent weapon that is used in a variety of fields, such as journalism, social media, government, and non-governmental organizations (NGOs). This chapter examines the practical uses of AI in these fields, emphasizing how AI-powered tools have been used to identify and counteract false information, validate news, influence legislation, and handle the particular difficulties faced by business stakeholders in a more hostile environment.

6.1 Artificial Intelligence in Social Media

Misinformation is primarily disseminated via social media sites like Facebook, Twitter, and YouTube. These platforms are now focal points for the employment of AI technology to identify and control fraudulent information because of their large user bases and ability to shape public opinion.

Automated Detection Tools for Facebook, Twitter, and YouTube

Manual moderation is impractical due to the volume and velocity of disinformation propagation on social media. These platforms have therefore included AI-powered technologies to help with content filtering and the identification of messages that are damaging, misleading, or deceptive.

- AI-Powered Content Moderation on Facebook: Facebook uses a variety of artificial intelligence (AI) models, such as natural language processing (NLP) and deep learning, to identify offensive content. By examining both text and graphics, the platform use these models to detect hate speech, fake news, and other types of damaging information. For instance, NLP models examine the text to find false narratives, while Facebook's image recognition algorithms can recognize photos or videos that have been altered.

- Fact-Checking Collaborations: To add more levels of inspection, Facebook has teamed up with outside fact-checkers. AI tools are used by these organizations, such as PolitiFact and Full Fact, to detect inaccurate material and confirm the content's legitimacy.

- Real-Time Misinformation Detection on Twitter: To identify and stop the spread of false information, Twitter has created a number of automatic tools that keep an eye on conversations in real time. In order to detect coordinated disinformation efforts, their AI models monitor viral content by examining user behavior and engagement metrics in addition to tweet content.

- Bot Detection: Finding automated bots that are frequently used to spread false information has been one of Twitter's main priorities. To differentiate bots from real human accounts, the platform uses machine learning algorithms to examine user activity patterns, including tweet frequency and language usage.

- Moderation of Video Content on YouTube: YouTube detects and flags potentially deceptive videos using AI-powered techniques. Videos that feature deepfakes, conspiracies, or inaccurate health information are among the things that the platform's content recognition technologies look for in order to identify content that violates community guidelines. Additionally, YouTube's algorithms give preference to content that can endanger public health or safety, such false information on COVID-19.

- Community Contributions: YouTube also depends on its user base to flag offensive material. AI algorithms then evaluate these reports and assist in ranking the instances for human moderators.

Openness and Algorithmic Responsibility

Even with the progress made in AI-powered content

Truth Decoded

moderation, accountability and transparency continue to be major obstacles. Users regularly express worry over the opacity of the algorithms that determine what content is tagged or removed. There is also an ongoing debate concerning algorithmic bias and the impact of these decisions on freedom of speech.

- Transparency Initiatives: Social media companies have started to move toward greater transparency in their AI algorithms in response to mounting public pressure. Facebook and Twitter, for example, now release yearly transparency reports that detail the amount of content that their AI algorithms have identified and eliminated, as well as the measures implemented against people who disseminate false information.

- Algorithmic Accountability: The possibility of algorithmic bias the notion that AI systems may unjustly single out particular opinions or groups is a major worry with regard to AI content moderation. In order to counteract this, businesses are spending money on research to make their models more accurate and equitable. They are also working with outside groups and independent auditors to examine their algorithms and make sure they are not perpetuating prejudices.

6.2 Resources for Journalism and News Verification

AI is increasingly being incorporated into journalistic workflows to help with fact-checking and news verification, as journalism plays a critical role in confirming facts and thwarting misinformation.

Verification Assisted by AI in Newsrooms

By automating labor-intensive and time-consuming processes, artificial intelligence is improving the verification process in newsrooms. AI tools assist journalists in rapidly evaluating the reliability of sources, confirming assertions, and identifying manipulated media because of the massive amount of content that is generated every day.

Fact-Checking AI Tools:

AI-powered platforms are made to check the accuracy of news stories, social media posts, and multimedia content by cross-referencing them with reliable sources. By promptly highlighting any disparities and anomalies, these technologies might give reporters leads for more research. An artificial intelligence program called ClaimBuster, created by researchers at the University of Texas, for instance, automatically recognizes factual statements in political discourse and verifies them against reliable sources.

- Natural Language Processing for Verification: Algorithms for natural language processing (NLP) are very helpful for examining vast amounts of textual material to find false or deceptive claims. Artificial intelligence (AI) systems, for instance, can be trained to identify the warning indicators of misinformation in publications, such as dramatic language, deceptive headlines, or selectively presented data.

Illustrations: ClaimReview, PolitiFact, and Full Fact

AI has been successfully incorporated into the verification procedures of a number of fact-checking groups.

- Full Fact: AI tools are used by Full Fact, an independent fact-checking nonprofit with headquarters in the UK, to help identify statements that are ready for fact-checking. These programs evaluate public leaders' statements and compare them to data from credible sources to assess their veracity. Real-time fact-checking of media reporting and political speeches has been made possible thanks in large part to Full Fact's AI capabilities.

- PolitiFact: Another well-known fact-checking group, PolitiFact, tracks the assertions made by public personalities and politicians using artificial intelligence. In order to assist journalists concentrate on the most important topics in real time, PolitiFact uses machine learning to classify and rank assertions for verification.

- ClaimReview: Google created the program, which enables fact-checkers and news organizations to annotate articles with information indicating whether a claim has been confirmed or refuted. Users may determine whether the content they are consuming has been fact-checked thanks to the integration of this metadata into search engines.

6.3 Use Cases for Government and NGO

In particular, when it comes to elections, public health, and policy creation, governments and non-governmental organizations are essential in combating disinformation. These days, AI-powered solutions are being used to create more successful intervention plans and enhance the reaction to disinformation.

AI-Powered Intervention and Policy Techniques

AI is being used by governments all around the world to improve their capacity to recognize and counteract false information.

Health Promotion Initiatives:

For instance, AI technologies were used to monitor the

dissemination of false information about the virus and vaccines during the COVID-19 epidemic. AI-powered systems were utilized by governments and health groups to scan social media for false information, identify trends, and reply with factual, evidence-based information.

- Election Security: To identify disinformation efforts meant to sway voters, governments have used AI-driven systems during elections. By analyzing social media and news platform trends, these systems are able to spot phony accounts and coordinated attempts to propagate misleading information. Governments have occasionally intervened to block or restrict access to such content.

International Partnerships to Combat Misinformation

The battle against disinformation is a worldwide issue that needs international collaboration and is not exclusive to any one government or organization. To combat the pervasive issue of fake news, a number of cooperative initiatives have been formed.

The EU Disinformation Code of Practice:

In an effort to stop the dissemination of false information, the European Union created the Code of Practice on Disinformation, which unites governments, non-governmental organizations, and digital corporations. AI is essential to this effort because it facilitates the large-scale detection and mitigation of misinformation.

Global Network of Fact-Checking:

A global effort to promote cooperation among fact-checking groups is the International Fact-Checking Network (IFCN). These organizations employ AI to validate claims and give the public accurate information by combining resources and expertise.

6.4 Industry Difficulties and Takeaways

Even with the remarkable advancements in AI-based disinformation detection, there are still a number of issues, mostly related to system resilience, false positives, and ethical issues.

Ethics, False Positives, and System Robustness

- System Robustness: The robustness of the systems itself is one of the main obstacles to employing AI for disinformation detection. It can be challenging for AI algorithms to correctly identify every instance of bogus content because misinformation can be subtle, complicated, and context-dependent. As misinformation strategies change, detection systems must likewise constantly adjust to new deceptive techniques.

- The term false positives refers to the occurrence of real content being flagged as false by AI systems. When speech and freedom of expression are at risk, these mistakes can be very harmful. Companies are attempting to improve their algorithms in order to lessen the frequency of false positives and guarantee that valid information is not mistakenly detected.

- Ethical Considerations: The use of AI for content moderation raises ethical questions as well, mainly in relation to algorithmic bias, censorship, and privacy. To keep the public's trust, AI systems must be impartial, transparent, and equitable.

Constant Adjustment under Harsh Circumstances

- AI-driven systems must be able to adjust to the ever-changing disinformation situation. Deepfakes and coordinated disinformation campaigns are examples of misinformation methods that are getting more complex, therefore detection systems need to be upgraded frequently to keep up with the latest developments.

- Learning from Failures: Constant feedback loops are necessary to combat the ongoing conflict between those who spread false information and those who defend AI. Numerous businesses and organizations have improved their systems and tactics throughout time by learning important lessons from past mistakes.

AI has shown itself to be a vital weapon in the battle against false information in a variety of fields, including government organizations and social media sites. We can develop more reliable, scalable, and efficient algorithms for identifying and thwarting bogus news by fusing AI with human knowledge. But as the difficulties change

It is imperative that ethical considerations continue to be at the forefront of the development and application of AI technologies, and that these technologies undergo constant adaptation. While the battle against false information is far from ended, artificial intelligence presents a bright future

CHAPTER 7

MODEL LIMITATIONS AND ADVERSARIAL THREATS

The way we tackle issues like content filtering and disinformation detection has been completely transformed by artificial intelligence (AI) systems. But the quick development of AI technology has also brought forth a number of serious problems, mostly due to model limits and hostile threats. These problems have the potential to compromise AI models' dependability, equity, and capacity to adjust to emerging dangers, thus undermining their very efficacy. This chapter will discuss the main adversarial risks that AI systems must contend with, the shortcomings of existing models, and how these issues affect the precision of disinformation detection. In order to maintain their dependability and credibility in the face of changing dangers, we will also examine the necessity for more resilient, transparent, and explicable AI systems.

7.1 Adversarial AI System Attacks

One of the biggest problems facing AI models, especially those employed in the identification of false information, is adversarial attacks. By purposefully altering AI models to generate inaccurate or deceptive results, these attacks compromise the models' capacity to function efficiently.

Using Adversarial Inputs to Modify Models

Adversarial attacks usually include making little, undetectable changes to the input data, which can lead to AI systems misinterpreting or incorrectly classifying the data. These modifications, referred to as adversarial inputs, are made expressly to take advantage of flaws in a model's algorithms.

Adversarial Inputs Example:

Adversarial inputs in the context of misinformation detection could include minor edits to a text or image that make it impossible for an AI system to recognize it as damaging or incorrect. An AI computer may be tricked into deeming a false news story as legitimate by making small changes to the sentence structure or word choice.

The effect on AI models

Adversarial attacks can make AI models vulnerable and unreliable, which is their primary problem. The model may provide erroneous outputs when an adversarial input is introduced into the system, seriously impairing its capacity to identify false information or carry out other tasks. In high-stakes settings where false information can spread quickly, such as newsrooms or social media platforms, this can have major repercussions.

Effects on Reliability of Detection

The caliber of the data used to train AI systems has a significant impact on their capacity to recognize false information. A basic flaw in existing models is revealed by adversarial attacks: they are vulnerable to inputs intended to trick them. These assaults have the potential to reduce AI model reliability in a number of ways:

- Loss of Confidence in Detection Systems: A system's ability to identify fake content may be compromised by adversarial inputs on a regular basis, which could cause users to lose faith in the technology. This undermines confidence in the system's capacity to identify valid judgments, particularly when identifying subtle types of false information.

- Adversarial attacks have the potential to produce false negatives, or situations in which damaging or deceptive content is not marked for review, in automated content moderation systems. This makes it possible for false information to evade detection and could have serious consequences.

7.2 Fake News Producers' Evasion Strategies

The strategies employed by disseminators of false information change along with AI systems. Malicious actors and producers of fake news have created complex strategies to avoid being discovered by AI-powered content moderation tools.

Algorithm gaming and content obscuration

- In an effort to evade AI detection, content producers who wish to manipulate algorithms have created a number of evasion strategies. These methods may entail minor content changes, which makes it more challenging for AI models to identify trends that point to false information.

- Content Obfuscation: Practitioners of fake news frequently use obfuscation techniques, which are tactics that purposefully conceal or change the actual meaning of content in ways that make it more difficult for AI models to understand. This could involve introducing distracting features into content that deceives AI systems, utilizing coded language, or randomly arranging phrase structures.

- Algorithm Gaming: In addition to obfuscation, proponents of false news also manipulate the algorithms used by AI models to categorize material, a practice known as algorithm gaming. To increase the visibility of their content, they can, for example, bombard social media sites with deceptive headlines or coordinate attempts to produce phony engagement (likes, shares, and retweets). Because of its seeming popularity, this deceives AI systems into identifying the content as more authentic.

Complex Storyline Manipulation

The complexity of narrative manipulation strategies employed by disinformation producers makes the problem much more difficult. These strategies entail creating false narratives that seem real and trustworthy, frequently through the use of selective data, emotional appeal, and misleading framing.

- Framing and Emotional Appeal: To influence public opinion, fake news producers frequently use emotionally charged language. Artificial intelligence (AI) systems, especially those that use sentiment analysis, could find it difficult to distinguish between honest emotional content and purposefully false tales meant to arouse anger, fear, or pity.

- Selective Fact-Checking: Offering cherry-picked

facts that promote a specific goal while disregarding context or contradicting data is another strategy known as selective use of facts. AI systems may find it challenging to identify these tales as deceptive, particularly when the content initially seems reliable.

7.3 Unintended Consequences and Model Bias

The problem of model bias has emerged as AI systems become more integrated into the battle against false information. Unintended effects might arise from bias in AI algorithms, especially when it comes to content detection and filtering.

Concerns about Censorship and Bias Amplification

Large datasets are used to train AI models, however these datasets frequently contain biases that the algorithms may unintentionally reinforce. These biases have the potential to intensify already-existing disparities or give rise to new types of discrimination in content moderation systems if they are not appropriately addressed.

- Bias Amplification: An AI model is likely to reinforce biases if it is trained on data that contains partial or biased information. An AI system that flags misleading content, for instance, can unfairly target some individuals, ideologies, or forms of misinformation while neglecting to sufficiently address others. As a result, the model's fairness and dependability are compromised and reality is distorted.

- Censorship Concerns: The possibility of over-censorship the propensity of AI models to flag or restrict content that may not necessarily be harmful or false is another problem with biased AI systems. This may result in content being unfairly removed or restricted, stifling valid voices and viewpoints that the algorithm could misunderstand.

Access to Appeal, Fairness, and Representation

Preventing unforeseen repercussions in AI systems requires ensuring justice and representation. It is crucial that AI models are made to be as objective as possible so that a range of viewpoints and information can be appropriately assessed.

- Algorithmic Decision-Making Fairness: Testing AI systems for bias and fairness is becoming more and more important, especially in the areas of disinformation detection and content moderation. Diverse datasets, frequent audits, and human supervision can all be used to help make sure AI models don't disproportionately target particular populations or reinforce negative preconceptions.

- Access to Appeal: Giving people the option to appeal AI-driven decisions is one method to overcome the fairness issue. In addition to giving content producers a say in the process, this allows people to analyze AI model decisions and offer context and subtleties that the system might have overlooked.

7.4 Requirement for Sturdy and Open AI Models

The demand for strong and transparent AI models that can

resist hostile attacks, reduce biases, and give concise justifications for their choices is increasing in order to meet the issues mentioned in the preceding sections. To foster confidence and guarantee that AI systems continue to be accountable, transparency and interpretability are essential.

Model Interpretability and Explainability

In addition to producing precise results, AI systems must also be able to justify their methods. The goal of the discipline of Explainable AI (XAI) is to develop models whose judgments are intelligible and interpretable by people.

- Why Explainability Is Important: Gaining the trust of stakeholders and users requires explainable AI. Users are more inclined to trust an AI model's recommendations and judgments if they comprehend how it comes to them. This is particularly crucial in delicate areas like content filtering, where users might contest the system's fairness.

- Model Interpretability: AI models need to be

comprehensible in order to be genuinely useful. This implies that their decision-making procedure ought to be open and transparent so that users and human moderators may comprehend the reasons behind the removal or flagging of a certain piece of material. AI systems can promote accountability and guarantee that choices are made in accordance with moral principles by offering this degree of transparency.

Increasing User Trust via Openness

A key element of the effective implementation of AI systems is trust. Users may grow doubtful about AI models in the absence of accountability and transparency, which could lower user engagement and undermine system trust.

- Building Trust: To gain the trust of users, organizations must place a high priority on transparency and clear communication. This involves giving thorough details about the data that AI models use, how they are trained, and how they operate. Regular audits of AI systems are also necessary to evaluate their effectiveness and resolve any concerns with bias, fairness, or transparency.

In the battle against false information, adversarial risks and model restrictions pose serious obstacles for AI systems. The dependability, equity, and transparency of AI-powered content moderation systems can be jeopardized by risks ranging from hostile attacks to evasion tactics and model bias. Building more resilient, transparent, and interpretable models that can handle these difficulties is crucial as AI technologies advance. We can only guarantee that AI continues to be a useful weapon in the fight against false information while preserving user confidence by resolving these issues

CHAPTER 8

PRIVACY, ETHICS, AND LEGAL ASPECTS

AI's use in information control and disinformation detection presents serious ethical, privacy, and legal issues as it continues to influence industries and daily life. It's not easy to strike the correct balance between the protection of fundamental rights like privacy and freedom of speech with technical improvements. The ethical ramifications of AI use in information control, privacy concerns related to data collecting, the changing legal and regulatory environment, and the fundamental ideas that direct the creation of moral AI systems are all covered in this chapter. The goal is to give a comprehensive grasp of the issues at hand and the factors that must be taken into account to guarantee the appropriate use of AI.

8.1 Information Control Using AI Ethically

Numerous ethical concerns are brought up by AI's use in

information regulation, especially in the area of misinformation detection. Although AI can greatly increase the speed and precision of detecting hazardous or deceptive content, its application needs to be done carefully to prevent unforeseen repercussions. It takes careful consideration to make sure AI tools are used ethically, especially when it comes to striking a balance between security, public safety, and individual liberties.

Finding a Balance Between Freedom of Speech and Safety

Finding a balance between safety and freedom of speech is one of the main ethical conundrums in the application of AI in information control. On the one hand, artificial intelligence (AI) can be used to weed out offensive or misleading material that could disseminate incorrect information, encourage violence, or do harm. However, excessively broad or oppressive methods may suppress free speech and hinder reasonable debate.

The Freedom of Expression:

Preventing the dissemination of false information and

damaging content is vital, but defending people's freedom of speech is just as vital. Overly strict content censorship by AI models may unintentionally stifle reasonable discussion and public debate. For instance, even though satire or political opinions aren't actually dangerous or deceptive, an AI system may flag them as such.

What Constitutes Harmful Content:

Another problem is figuring out what exactly qualifies as "harmful" information. Diverse cultures, geographical areas, and people may hold differing opinions about what constitutes injury. For example, what is considered hate speech in one nation may be considered a valid form of political expression or protest in another. This intricacy makes it more challenging to develop AI systems that successfully strike a balance between free expression and safety without going too far.

Preventing Overuse and Abuse of Detection Instruments

AI has the potential to be a very effective tool for weeding out false information, but it may also be abused and overused. The danger is that AI systems may be utilized for corporate, social, or political control, which would result in the repression of knowledge that contradicts the current quo.

- Censorship and Algorithmic Bias: AI systems can only be as objective as the data they are trained on. The system's decisions will be biased if there are inherent biases in the training data. Content that does not fit into a specific political or ideological viewpoint may be censored as a result, even if it is not intrinsically damaging.

- Lack of Transparency: Another major issue is the opacity of many AI systems. It becomes challenging to guarantee that AI-driven judgments about content moderation are handled impartially and fairly when they are made behind closed doors without transparent justification or accountability. Without a clear explanation of how or why specific content was detected or removed, users and content creators may feel that their rights are being infringed.

8.2 Privacy Issues with Data Gathering

The efficiency of AI in content moderation and disinformation detection frequently depends on having access to vast volumes of personal data. Social media activity, browser patterns, search history, and even private chats can all be included in this data. There are serious privacy concerns raised by the gathering, storing, and usage of this data.

Consent, Anonymity, and Surveillance Hazards

The issues of anonymity and consent are central to privacy problems. A large number of users might not completely comprehend or agree to the gathering of their data for the purposes of disinformation identification or AI-driven content moderation. This brings up important moral questions about accountability, transparency, and user rights.

- Surveillance Concerns: AI systems that use large datasets frequently entail a great deal of surveillance of people's online activity. The accuracy of disinformation detection may be improved by this surveillance, but there is a chance that users' feeling of privacy and autonomy may be compromised by invasive monitoring. For example, monitoring someone's social connections or political opinions may be considered a privacy violation, particularly if the information is used to sway choices or actions.

- Informed Consent: Users' informed consent should be obtained before AI systems can gather and use data. Many platforms, however, gather data without making adequate disclosures, so consumers are ignorant of how their data is being utilized. In order to provide people choice over how their data is shared and utilized in AI applications, consent needs to be clear, informed, and revocable.

GDPR and Procedures for Data Protection

One of the most extensive privacy regulations to handle data protection issues is the General Data Protection Regulation (GDPR), which was put into effect in the European Union. Important guidelines for the collection, storage, and use of personal data have been established by the GDPR, particularly when AI systems are involved.

- Data Minimization: Organizations are required by the GDPR to follow the principle of data minimization, making sure that they only gather the data required for the intended purpose. Given the potential drawbacks of big datasets, this is especially crucial for AI applications. Although they increase model accuracy, they also raise the possibility of privacy violations and data exploitation.

- One of the most important features of the GDPR is the right to explanation, which gives people the right to know how automated decisions like those pertaining to content moderation are made. This emphasizes the need for transparency in the way AI systems handle and use personal data, which is in line with the growing desire for explainable AI.

8.3 The Regulatory and Legal Environment

Governments throughout the world are finding it difficult

to keep up with the quick speed at which technology is advancing, and the legal environment surrounding AI is constantly evolving. As AI is increasingly incorporated into content control and misinformation detection, it is important to comprehend the changing legal and regulatory frameworks that regulate its use.

Reactions of National and International Policies

A fragmented landscape of national and international regulations is the outcome of different nations' differing approaches to AI regulation. While some countries are currently creating frameworks, others have already put AI-specific laws into effect.

- European Union: The AI Act is one of the most extensive pieces of law designed to ensure the responsible use of AI, and the European Union has been a global leader in AI regulation. With a focus on openness, responsibility, and equity, the legislation specifies certain standards for AI systems employed in high-risk domains like content moderation and disinformation detection.

- The regulatory environment in the United States is more dispersed, with state and federal laws controlling misinformation, AI ethics, and data privacy. However, the lack of a single, all-encompassing AI regulation results in uneven enforcement and a lack of clarity surrounding the legal responsibilities of businesses that use AI systems for content management.

AI's Function in Digital Rights and Legal Accountability

AI will have a big impact on how legal accountability and digital rights develop in the future. Determining legal accountability for AI-driven choices are becoming more and more necessary as AI systems become more integrated into the administration of justice, privacy, and individual rights.

- Liability and Accountability: When an AI system makes a biased or incorrect choice, who bears the blame? For instance, who is responsible for any potential harm if an AI system incorrectly flags a piece of content as harmful? This concern is especially pertinent when AI judgments violate people's rights or cause harm to one's reputation.

- Ensuring the protection of digital rights: Protecting digital rights, including the right to privacy, the right to free speech, and the right to access information, has grown more important in an increasingly digital society. Strong legal frameworks and effective enforcement methods are necessary to guarantee that these rights are upheld as AI systems get more involved in content moderation.

8.4 Developing Moral AI Frameworks

Developers and stakeholders must follow specific guidelines while creating and implementing AI systems to guarantee that these technologies are used sensibly and morally. Developing ethical AI is not only a technical problem but also a moral requirement, particularly in delicate fields like content regulation and misinformation detection.

Ethical AI Design Principles

Fairness, accountability, openness, and privacy should be the main tenets of ethical AI design. The development process and the final result are shaped by these principles, which are more than just idealistic concepts.

- Fairness: AI systems that are ethical must be built with fairness and little bias in mind. This involves making sure that particular groups, beliefs, or individuals are not unfairly discriminated against by the system's outputs. Fairness in AI decision-making can be ensured with the support of routine testing and audits.

- Transparency: The way AI systems make decisions should be open and honest. This involves giving users concise explanations of the decision-making process and enabling them to comprehend the justification for actions such as content control or misinformation detection.

- Accountability: Companies and developers are responsible for the behavior of their AI systems. This entails developing mechanisms that enable supervision and recourse, guaranteeing that choices made by AI systems may be examined and, if needed, adjusted.

- Privacy: AI systems should be developed with privacy in mind, guaranteeing the protection of user privacy and the rights of users to manage their own data.

Including Stakeholders in the Development of Systems

It takes cooperation from a variety of stakeholders, including developers, legislators, and the general public, to create ethical AI. Incorporating a variety of viewpoints into the development process guarantees that the system is created with equity, openness, and responsibility in mind and covers a wide range of issues.

Teamwork Approach:

AI systems can be developed with a more comprehensive

grasp of the possible hazards and societal effects by including ethicists, legal professionals, civil society organizations, and users in the process. This cooperative strategy aids in guaranteeing that AI technologies uphold individual rights while serving the public interest.

AI's role in content moderation and disinformation detection raises a number of intricate and multidimensional ethical, privacy, and legal issues. It is crucial to make sure that AI is created and used ethically since it will continue to have a significant impact on how information is shared and controlled. Building AI systems that are not only efficient but also equitable, open, and accountable will require balancing safety, privacy, and free speech, addressing the changing regulatory environment, and abiding by ethical standards

CHAPTER 9

PROSPECTS FOR AI-POWERED DETECTION IN THE FUTURE

The potential of artificial intelligence (AI) to improve human capacity to recognize, evaluate, and stop the spread of false information is growing along with the field of disinformation detection. Although AI-powered detection systems have advanced significantly thus far, even more revolutionary potential lies ahead. In addition to the adaptable and constantly changing AI models that will revolutionize how we combat disinformation in an increasingly complex digital ecosystem, this chapter examines the new technologies and breakthroughs that will influence the next generation of misinformation detection. We also look at the possibility of human-machine cooperation and the significance of creating international tactics to counter false information.

9.1 New Innovations and Technologies

AI is developing at an astounding rate, and new discoveries are made on a regular basis. Transformers, multimodal AI, and zero-shot learning are some of the most promising technologies for improving AI-powered detection systems. Furthermore, combining AI with blockchain and decentralized technologies may provide fresh approaches to guaranteeing data openness and integrity in the battle against false information.

Zero-Shot Learning, Multimodal AI, and Transformers

Historically, AI models have made predictions using pre-existing datasets. But because of transformer models like GPT and BERT, AI is now much better at comprehending relationships, context, and subtleties in big datasets. These models may produce extremely accurate predictions for a range of tasks, including disinformation detection, and can process enormous volumes of data.

- Transformers: Unlike conventional sequential models, transformer models allow text data to be processed in parallel, revolutionizing natural language processing (NLP). This development makes it possible for AI systems to comprehend word-phrase interactions more deeply, which makes them extremely useful for identifying subtle types of disinformation like context manipulation or deceptive headlines. Transformers perform exceptionally well on tasks that call for knowledge of both individual words and the larger context of a sentence or paragraph, which is essential for spotting inaccurate or deceptive content.

- Multimodal AI: To produce more thorough insights, multimodal AI refers to systems that combine and process many data kinds, including text, images, audio, and video. Multimodal AI can be used to cross-check information across several media types in the context of disinformation detection, increasing accuracy and spotting misleading content that may include text, photos, and videos. An AI system might, for instance, identify a movie as having modified images while simultaneously looking for inconsistencies or false statements in the text that goes with it.

- Zero-Shot Learning: This technique enables AI systems to identify and comprehend tasks without prior explicit training on particular samples. This method is particularly useful for disinformation detection since it allows AI models to recognize previously undiscovered forms of misinformation or content modification strategies. AI systems can stay ahead of changing strategies for disseminating misleading information by utilizing zero-shot learning, which guarantees that their efficacy will not diminish as disinformation tactics evolve.

Blockchain and Decentralized Technology Integration

In the digital era, blockchain technology, which is well-known for producing clear, impenetrable records, may be crucial in enhancing the reliability of data. We could build a more robust infrastructure for confirming the legitimacy of digital information by combining blockchain and decentralized technology with AI-powered detection systems.

Transparency and Verification Blockchain:

- Because of its transparency, blockchain is a perfect tool for confirming the legitimacy and provenance of information. AI algorithms would be able to quickly track the origin of information and identify any instances of manipulation or alteration if all content were recorded on a decentralized ledger. An image or video's history, for example, may be tracked by a blockchain, enabling AI to verify whether it has been altered or used misleadingly.

- Decentralized Content Moderation: The task of content moderation may be divided across decentralized networks. Decentralized systems might leverage AI to crowdsource the identification of false information from a diverse range of individuals, each of whom would contribute to the moderation process, rather than depending on centralized platforms to regulate the flow of information. Because this methodology takes into account a wider range of viewpoints and data sources, it may lessen bias and improve the overall efficacy of misinformation detection.

9.2 Models of Adaptive and Continuous Learning

The issue known as concept drift, in which the features of disinformation change over time, is one of the persistent problems in misinformation detection. AI models must swiftly adjust to new forms of misleading information in order to continue to be useful. In order to overcome this difficulty and develop more individualized and responsive detection systems, this part investigates the use of adaptive and continuous learning models.

Handling Concept Drift and Changing Falsehoods

When an AI model's learnt patterns deteriorate over time as a result of shifting data distribution, this is known as concept drift. This implies that the strategies employed to disseminate misleading information will change over time, necessitating rapid adaptation of AI systems to emerging dangers.

- Continuous Model Training: Using continuous training procedures is one way to counteract concept drift. The system can continue to be accurate and relevant by providing AI models with current data, including fresh examples of false information. This could entail dynamically modifying the model's parameters utilizing real-time data streams or retraining models on a regular basis with new instances of false information. To keep the models up to date with the latest misinformation trends, AI systems might be trained on content that has been identified as misleading by credible sources, such as journalists or fact-checkers.

- Dynamic Detection Strategies: AI systems are also capable of implementing dynamic detection techniques, which change in reaction to novel disinformation patterns. For example, AI models can provide new methods for recognizing altered media and deepfakes as they become more common. AI may be trained to identify new deception techniques as they appear by emphasizing dynamic learning, which keeps detection tools current.

Customized Detection Mechanisms

In misinformation detection, personalization entails adjusting AI models to suit certain users or situations. By taking into account the distinct requirements, habits, and interests of the audience, personalized systems can increase the precision and applicability of misinformation identification.

- User-Centric Detection: Tailored AI systems may examine a person's social media behavior, surfing preferences, and consumption patterns to identify false content that is especially pertinent to them. In addition to improving detection accuracy, this strategy would enable more focused interventions, including warnings or instructional messages meant to assist users in critically assessing the content they come across.

- Aware of Context Detection: Context-aware systems would take into account the particular context in which information is being exchanged or consumed, in addition to individual customizing. This can entail being aware of the subtle political, social, or cultural factors that influence how false information is interpreted and disseminated. Context-aware detection algorithms would be better equipped to spot deceptive content in particular circumstances and offer more thoughtful answers, making sure that interventions are suitable for the target audience and the relevant data.

9.3 Cooperation Between Machines and People

Even while AI has shown great promise in identifying false information, it is unlikely to completely replace people in this process. The future of disinformation detection will instead depend on augmented intelligence, a paradigm in which artificial intelligence (AI) complements and improves human judgment rather than taking its place. The possibility of human-machine cooperation in the continuous fight against disinformation is examined in this section.

Augmented Intelligence: AI Aiding Humans, Not Taking Their Place

Instead of serving as self-sufficient substitutes, augmented intelligence centers on the notion that AI technologies can improve human decision-making. This means that by automating the process of content analysis and identifying possible disinformation for more research, AI can assist human fact-checkers, journalists, and media organizations in the context of misinformation identification.

- AI as a Tool for Journalists: Journalists can use AI-powered tools to fact-check statements, swiftly identify and evaluate the reliability of sources, and track the dissemination of misleading information. By offering real-time statistics on the virality of material or pointing out new trends in disinformation, artificial intelligence (AI) could help journalists keep ahead of misleading narratives.

- Automated Decisions with Human Oversight: Even with AI's skills, human supervision is still crucial. Before rendering a final decision, people must consider the context and subtleties, even when AI systems may flag content as potentially misleading. We can prevent AI-driven systems from functioning in a vacuum or developing biases in their evaluations by preserving human participation in the decision-making process.

Collaborating with Journalists and Citizens to Develop Detection Tools

- Developing more ethical and efficient disinformation detection systems will require cooperation from citizens, journalists, and AI developers. We can make sure that detection tools are based on practical experience and are sensitive to the needs of people who depend on them by incorporating a variety of stakeholders in their development.

- Identifying False Information through Crowdsourcing: Misinformation detection systems can be made more accurate by utilizing the collective intelligence of the people. Together with AI technologies, citizen-led initiatives can assist in locating and confirming content from news sources and social media platforms. By addressing the issues and values of many communities, this cooperative approach may also help guarantee that detecting systems continue to be democratic and inclusive.

9.4 Moving Forward with a Worldwide Misinformation Defense Plan

Misinformation transcends national boundaries in a world growing more interconnected by the day. **Global** initiatives that encourage cross-border cooperation and guarantee the preservation of digital rights will be necessary for the future of disinformation detection. The potential for international data sharing and cross-border activities to create more robust and efficient information ecosystems is examined in this section.

Global Data Sharing and Cross-Border Initiatives

Since misinformation frequently spreads quickly across national borders, preventing its spread requires a global approach. Global cooperation can improve the efficacy and reach of disinformation detection systems, guaranteeing the preservation of information integrity everywhere.

- worldwide Networks for disinformation Monitoring: Private businesses, governments, and international organizations can collaborate to create worldwide networks for disinformation monitoring and countering. These networks can produce a more cohesive response to international disinformation operations by exchanging information on new dangers, working together on research, and coordinating activities across national borders.

- The flow of information required to monitor and counteract misinformation may be facilitated by Data-Sharing Agreements between nations and organizations. These agreements might make it possible to share data on misinformation trends in real time, which would aid in spotting new false narratives before they become widely accepted.

Constructing Robust Information Environments

Constructing a robust

Creating an atmosphere that allows reliable, correct information to flourish is known as the information ecology. This calls for infrastructure that encourages the appropriate use of information, media literacy, education, and sophisticated detection mechanisms.

- Advancing Digital Knowledge: Investing in digital literacy instruction is essential to creating resilient information ecosystems. We can empower people to make informed decisions and lessen the impact of disinformation by educating them how to critically analyze sources, identify bias, and determine the reliability of information.

- Supporting Independent Journalism: Accurate information must be verified and disseminated by independent journalism. Establishing a reliable information environment requires backing media companies that uphold strict integrity and transparency requirements. AI and human journalists can collaborate to make it harder for false information to spread.

AI-powered detection systems have a bright future. We can create a stronger defense against false information by adopting new technologies, adaptive learning models, human-machine collaboration, and international initiatives. The path ahead will necessitate ongoing innovation, careful cooperation, and a dedication to creating robust, open information ecosystems that support accountability and the truth in the digital era

CHAPTER 10

FINAL THOUGHTS - OUTLINING THE FUTURE

Information is now more convenient and accessible than ever thanks to the digital era, but it also brings with it the constant problem of false information. In the fight against fake news, artificial intelligence (AI) has become a potent weapon as well as a driving force behind new types of dishonesty. It is evident from considering the developments in AI-driven disinformation detection that combating fake news calls for a cooperative, interdisciplinary strategy in addition to technology innovation. In order to overcome the continuous conflict between truth and false information in the digital age, this last chapter lays out a plan for the future.

10.1 Highlighting Important Takeaways

It's critical to highlight the key takeaways and revelations from this investigation as we draw to a close this voyage through the intricate realm of artificial intelligence and disinformation detection. With its capacity to swiftly scan enormous volumes of data, spot trends, and evaluate reliability in ways that humans cannot, artificial intelligence (AI) has unquestionably shown itself to be a potent weapon in the battle against fake news. But it's important to recognize these technologies' advantages as well as their drawbacks.

AI's Potential and Achievements

- Speed and Efficiency: Artificial intelligence (AI) systems are excellent at sorting through enormous amounts of data in real-time, enabling the near-instantaneous identification of false information. AI can examine text, photos, audio, and video for indications of manipulation, context distortion, and other types of deceptive content using machine learning algorithms. This effectiveness significantly speeds up the identification process and gives platforms and users real-time feedback.

- Pattern Recognition: The ability of AI to identify

intricate patterns in data is one of its most potent features. Artificial intelligence (AI) may recognize minor indicators of disinformation, such as fabricated claims, misleading imagery, and distorted headlines, using methods like natural language processing (NLP) and deep learning. As new types of false information appear, these systems can adjust to them, enhancing their detection power over time.

- Tackling Disinformation on a Large Scale: AI's scalability enables it to fight false information globally. It is simply impossible for humans to manually monitor and verify every piece of information due to the growing volume of content posted online, including news articles and social media posts. AI provides a crucial answer to this problem by offering automatic techniques for spotting and flagging potentially dangerous false information.

AI's Drawbacks

Even with its amazing potential, artificial intelligence has drawbacks. It's critical to acknowledge the obstacles that still prevent it from reaching its full potential in misinformation detection.

- Contextual Understanding: Although AI is good at seeing patterns, it still has trouble comprehending the larger context of information. For instance, it's still difficult to identify irony, cultural quirks, or emotional undertones in written material. When it comes to comprehending the social and political factors that influence the dissemination of false information, AI systems are frequently less trustworthy.

- AI systems are only as good as the data they are trained on, which leads to bias and false positives. The resulting AI model may reinforce biases if the training data is skewed or lacking, producing false positives or incorrect conclusions. This is especially troublesome when it comes to disinformation detection, as subtle distinctions between false and accurate content could be missed.

- Vulnerability to Adversarial Attacks: People who want to disseminate false information can manipulate AI systems. AI can be tricked into misclassifying content using adversarial assaults, which include making minor, intentional changes to input data in order to deceive the machine. These flaws emphasize how crucial it is to continuously improve AI detection systems and provide anti-exploitation measures.

10.2 Developing an interdisciplinary reaction

It takes cooperation from all facets of society to combat misinformation; it is not a one-sided endeavor. The development of a comprehensive response to fake news requires the participation of educators, technologists, legislators, and civic society. To counteract disinformation, a framework that is ethical, flexible, and resilient must be built using a multidisciplinary approach.

The Function of Teachers

At the core of the answer are educators. The proliferation

of false information has highlighted the importance of media literacy and critical thinking in the classroom. Teachers may contribute to creating a generation that is more resistant to false information by teaching students how to analyze sources, gauge reliability, and challenge the veracity of information.

- Media Literacy: In order to teach students how to handle the complexity of the digital world, schools and institutions must incorporate media literacy into their curricula. Pupils should be urged to consider the reliability of the material they come across, comprehend how algorithms affect the visibility of content, and identify the moral ramifications of disseminating incorrect information.

- Encouraging Critical Thinking: Teachers can also assist students in acquiring critical thinking abilities, which will allow them to evaluate and comprehend data from various angles. Students have the ability to identify prejudice, unearth covert motives, and comprehend the larger context of news articles as a result.

Technologists' Function

The development of AI and technology is essential to enhancing misinformation detection systems. In order to ensure that these technologies adapt to new trends in disinformation, it is their responsibility to keep improving the instruments and algorithms that aid in spotting fake news.

- Creating Ethical AI: Researchers need to create AI systems that are open, objective, and impervious to manipulation. Developing ethical AI should be a primary goal in order to make sure that these systems respect society's values and don't cause harm.

- Interdisciplinary Cooperation: To develop more advanced and accountable disinformation detection systems, cooperation between AI researchers, social scientists, and ethicists is crucial. Together, these professionals can guarantee that AI tools are morally and practically sound.

The Function of Lawmakers

Regulating the dissemination of false information while maintaining the protection of free speech is a critical task for policymakers. It is their duty to enact regulations and policies that hold platforms responsible for the content they carry while promoting free speech.

- **Creating Explicit Regulations:** To guarantee openness in content moderation procedures, governments should create thorough, explicit regulations for internet platforms. These rules ought to protect people's privacy and liberties while addressing the dissemination of false information.

- Supporting Fact-Checking Initiatives: Legislators ought to back independent fact-checking groups and give them money so they can continue their work. A vital component of the ecosystem, fact-checkers assist in spotting and disproving erroneous information that spreads online.

Civil Society's Function

The battle against disinformation also heavily relies on civil society organizations, such as advocacy groups, grassroots movements, and non-governmental organizations (NGOs).

- Public Awareness Campaigns: To warn the public about the risks of false information and how to recognize it, civil society organizations can spearhead public awareness campaigns. The goal of these programs should be to enable people to report fake news when they come across it and to be responsible information consumers.

- **Community Engagement:** Developing resilience against false information requires involving communities at the local level. Local groups can support the development of an information-sharing culture that prioritizes accountability and the truth, inspiring people to join the fight against false information.

10.3 Strengthening Users Against False Information

Giving users more power is one of the most crucial elements in the fight against false information. Even while legislation and technology are important, people are ultimately in charge of the information they produce, distribute, and consume. Digital empowerment, community involvement, and media literacy are essential elements of this endeavor.

Knowledge of Media

- Adult Education Programs: Although a lot of work has gone into teaching the younger generation, adults are just as susceptible to false information. Building a society capable of critically engaging with information can be greatly aided by public campaigns and workshops targeted at enhancing media literacy among adults.

- Using AI as a Tool for Empowerment: AI tools can be used to empower people to recognize false information on their own in addition to detecting fake news. We can provide individuals with the knowledge they need to defend themselves against false information by giving them access to tools that can evaluate the reliability of sources, verify facts, and evaluate content.

Interaction with the Community

- A self-regulating community can be established via platforms that encourage users to flag potentially inaccurate content. This is known as crowdsourcing misinformation detection. The collective wisdom of the community can assist in identifying erroneous content that might evade detection, hence crowdsourcing disinformation detection can greatly enhance the efforts of AI systems.

- Building Trust: Communities can develop trust around the information they exchange by cultivating an atmosphere of open communication and respect for one another. Because people are more inclined to believe and disseminate information from reliable sources, this trust can act as a buffer against false information.

10.4 The Veracity of Truth in the AI Age

The future of truth in the digital era is still up in the air as AI technologies develop further. We can, however, face this future with ethical optimism the conviction that we can overcome the obstacles that lie ahead if we apply careful consideration, teamwork, and a dedication to truth. Technology alone won't be enough to detect false information in the future; society as a whole must also be willing to put honesty and integrity first.

Moral Hopefulness

- A Well-Rounded Strategy: A balance between ethical responsibility and technological progress will be necessary in the future. AI has the potential to be a very positive force, but its development and application must be carefully considered to ensure that it supports democratic ideals and serves the public interest.

- Using AI to Promote Positive Change: The potential of AI goes far beyond identifying false information. It can be used to advance accountability, truth, and openness in all areas of life. We can anticipate a time when technology enhances human potential and advances society by making sure AI systems are consistent with these ideals.

Getting Ready for the Upcoming Information Warfare Wave

We must continue to be alert and proactive in our preparation for emerging kinds of disinformation and digital manipulation as AI technologies develop. Deepfakes and other types of deception, together with even more advanced AI-generated material, are expected to be hallmarks of the next generation of information warfare. We can make sure that truth wins in the era of artificial intelligence by foreseeing these difficulties and arming ourselves with the required resources, information, and frameworks.

In summary, cooperation, education, and moral innovation

are the ways to go forward. We can create a future where truth is not only safeguarded but also given the ability to flourish by utilizing the combined capabilities of technology, society, and humans.

ABOUT THE AUTHOR

 Author and thought leader in the IT field Taylor Royce is well known. He has a two-decade career and is an expert at tech trend analysis and forecasting, which enables a wide audience to understand complicated concepts.

Royce's considerable involvement in the IT industry stemmed from his passion with technology, which he developed during his computer science studies. He has extensive knowledge of the industry because of his experience in both software development and strategic consulting.

Known for his research and lucidity, he has written multiple best-selling books and contributed to esteemed tech periodicals. Translations of Royce's books throughout the world demonstrate his impact.

Royce is a well-known authority on emerging technologies

and their effects on society, frequently requested as a speaker at international conferences and as a guest on tech podcasts. He promotes the development of ethical technology, emphasizing problems like data privacy and the digital divide.

In addition, with a focus on sustainable industry growth, Royce mentors upcoming tech experts and supports IT education projects. Taylor Royce is well known for his ability to combine analytical thinking with technical know-how. He sees a time when technology will ethically benefit humanity.